MW00607134

*I*n our *carpe diem* state of mind, we decide to take a big risk and live by our wits. Travel will be tied to a bigger word, *freedom.*

—*A Year in the World*

This book belongs to:

_____

Excerpts are from the books by Frances
Mayes: *Under the Tuscan Sun* (copyright ©
1998), *Bella Tuscany: The Sweet Life in Italy*
(copyright © 1999), *A Year in the World:
Journeys of a Passionate Traveler* (copyright
© 2006), *Every Day in Tuscany: Seasons of
an Italian Life* (copyright © 2010).

POTTER STYLE

Text copyright © 2011 by Frances Mayes.
Jacket photographs copyright © 2011 by
Steven Rothfeld
Published in the United States by Potter
Style, an imprint of the Crown Publishing
Group, a division of Random House, Inc.,
New York. www.clarksonpotter.com
ISBN 978-0-307-72088-7

DESIGN BY James Massey
Printed in China

the Passionate Traveler Journal

*I*n 1990, our first summer in Tuscany, I bought an oversized blank book with Florentine paper covers and blue leather binding. On the first page I wrote ITALY. The book looked as though it should have immortal poetry in it, but I began with lists of wildflowers, lists of projects, new words, sketches of tile in Pompeii. I described rooms, trees, bird calls. I added planting advice: "Plant sunflowers when the moon crosses Libra," although I had no clue myself as to when that might be. I wrote about the people we met and the food we cooked.

*T*he book became a chronicle of our years together in Tuscany. Today it is stuffed with menus, postcards of paintings, a drawing of a floor plan of an abbey, Italian poems, and diagrams of the garden. Because it is thick, I still have room in it for a few more summers. Now the blue book has become *Under the Tuscan Sun*, a natural outgrowth of my first pleasures here. Restoring, then improving, the house; transforming an overgrown jungle into its proper function as a farm for olives and grapes; exploring the layers and layers of Tuscany and Umbria; cooking in a foreign kitchen and discovering the many links between the food and the culture—these intense joys frame the deeper pleasure of learning to live another kind of life. To bury the grape tendril in such a way that it shoots out new growth I recognize easily as a metaphor for the way life must change from time to time if we are to go forward in our thinking.

—Frances Mayes, *Under the Tuscan Sun*

Whatever a guidebook says, whether or not you leave somewhere with a sense of place is entirely a matter of smell and instinct.

—Under the Tuscan Sun

ITALY

In my "walking notebook": tile rooftops, a handmade ladder propped in a fig tree, olive trees beside a stone wall, a man outlined in a doorway—these images are contemporary or medieval or Roman and so partake of the timeless. A stone wall glinting in the wet light—what stone does to light speaks emblematically to a sense of time that floats from one era to the next. In a nimbus of gold, a little dirt-colored donkey stands against a whitewashed wall, a stony path winds into a smoky aura of light; a man with a birthmark covering half of his face tips his chair against the wall under the arbor and laughs; a distant tower seems to exist through a long telescope into time.

—A Year in the World

On the first day in a new place, it's good to wander, absorb colors, textures, and scents, see who lives here, and find the rhythm of the day. We'll crank into tourist mode later, making sure we don't miss the great sights.

—Bella Tuscany

FEZ, MOROCCO

The women flow in the impossibly narrow lanes, a river of color: saffron, burgundy, sage, pistachio, peacock blue, threading the crowds, Nile greens and mustard parting, rust, magenta, emerald merging, tomato red, ochre and all the earth colors, the occasional white worn by a woman in mourning. Some are secluded, occluded behind black veils, some wear modest scarves, and some neither. I see them look at me then quickly away.

—A Year in the World

When traveling, you have the delectable possibility of not understanding a word that is said to you. Language becomes simply a musical background for watching bicycles zoom along a canal, calling for nothing from you. Even better, if you speak the language, you catch nuances and make more contact with people.

—A Year in the World

ANDALUCÍA, SPAIN

I am going to Spain for a winter month in Andalucía. Andulacía, land of the orange and the olive tree. Land of passionate poets and flamenco dancers and late-night dinners with guitar music in jasmine-scented gardens.

—A Year in the World

Setting off to see another country, I set off to see what is more grandly other—whole cultures, geographies, languages. Who am I in the new place? And who are they who live there?

—Bella Tuscany

FRANCE

The French pastry shops—aqua, blue, or pink with gold letters—look like their own confections. The little bell rings, and you're welcomed into a tidy shop with buttery, warm smells wafting from the kitchen. The pastries are about form as well as taste. The rich puffs and ruffles and layers and colors form tasty morsels, but they also reward the eye.

—A Year in the World

ITALY

Italy is an immortal playground. Does any country come close to its sustained, heady concoction of joys—serene landscape and magnificent art and layered history and savory cuisine and glorious music and welcoming people? So many ands. All in an elongated peninsula slashed down the middle with mountains, packed and stacked with dialects, great cooks, the Renaissance, hill towns, evocative cinema, ruins, castles, mosaics, villas, church bells, beaches, and on and on. Just as we think we won't find anywhere to eat on this back road, a small osteria appears.

This is Italy . . .

—Every Day in Tuscany

PALERMO, SICILY

The freezers glow with sorbetti—*pistachio, lemon, watermelon, cinnamon, jasmine, almond, as well as the usual fruits. Most children seem to prefer gelato, not in a cup or cone, but stuffed inside a brioche. Just looking at the almond cake is almost enough satisfaction, but instead we split one of the crisp* cannoli *lined with chocolate and heavenly, creamy ricotta. No harm done; we're planning to walk for the rest of the afternoon.*

—Bella Tuscany

With the force of an earth-quake, a wild certainty forms in the center of my forehead. Time. To go. Time. Just go.

—A Year in the World

SCOTLAND

Falkland is downright obsessed with flowers. Wooden tubs and farm carts overflow with blooms, window boxes adorn even the humblest house, tumbling baskets hang along iron fences and from iron poles, all prolifically spilling with splendid yellow and orange begonias, trailing ivy, lobelia, and petunias. . . . In spring everyone rushes to a town plant sale.

—A Year in the World

LYCIAN COAST, TURKEY

In the Spice Bazaar we buy garam masala and strawberry tea. Bins are heaped with dill, mint, pistachios, curry, hot paprika, black chili, turmeric, hot peppers—all the colors in the rugs…We see mounds of various nuts, honeycombs dripping, heaps of dried apples, apricots, and figs—some look rather dusty. Lokum, the Turksih delight, appears in many sugary pastels.

—A Year in the World

When you travel, you become invisible, if you want. I do want. I like to be the observer. What makes these people who they are? Could I feel at home here? No one expects you to have a stack of papers back by Tuesday, or to check messages, or to fertilize the geraniums.

—A Year in the World

SINTRA, PORTUGAL

It's easy to see why a poet would be drawn to this craggy and forested landscape of palaces, secret gates, views of the sea, and mysterious fog pulled in from the water by the hotter interior. Moisture drips from trees, and the air makes you want to inhale. Not as fashionable as it once was, Sintra still has its share of hidden estates and a few shops for clothes and home décor. Of course it has a good bakery, a perfect place to try the local specialty, queijadas de Sintra, cheesecake tarts with a scent of Moorish cinnamon.

—A Year in the World

Travel releases spontaneity. You become a godlike creature full of choice, free to visit the stately pleasure domes, make love in the morning, sketch a bell tower, read a history of Byzantium, stare for one hour at the face of Leonardo da Vinci's Madonna dei fusi. *You open, as in childhood, and—for a time—receive this world. There's the visceral aspect, too—the huntress who is free. Free to go, free to return home bringing memories to lay on the hearth.*

—A Year in the World

My idea of heaven still
is to drive the gravel farm
roads of Umbria and Tus-
cany, very pleasantly lost.

—Under the Tuscan Sun

GREEK ISLANDS

At sea, the water is lighter than lapis. Endless blue, the bluest blue, forget-me-not blue. If only I could find a word to anneal to the blue, a lucid, gossamer word. The ship's bow raises a V of foam that folds over into the blue. I could stand on deck all day, just looking at this endless shift of patterning on the surface of the sea. Vinca, periwinkle——not quite. A lively blue, a wet enamel shine, a depth of blue. Sapphire——yes, that much play of light. A mystery with all the weight and expanse of land. In summer calm, exuberant.

—A Year in the World

The need to travel is a mysterious force. A desire to go runs through me equally with an intense desire to stay at home. An equal and opposite thermodynamic principle. When I travel, I think of home and what it means. At home I'm dreaming of catching trains at night in the gray light of Old Europe, or pushing open shutters to see Florence awaken. The balance just slightly tips in the direction of the airport.

—A Year in the World

Meandering around several villages and visiting two gardens fills a day. After pub lunches, we have salad and cheese at night back at our schoolhouse, treating ourselves to bowls of prime strawberries with double cream for dessert.

—A Year in the World

It's not the destinations; it's the ability to be on the road, happy trails, out where no one knows or understands or cares about all the deviling things that have been weighing you down, keeping you frantic as a lizard with a rock on its tail.

—Under the Tuscan Sun

CAPRI, ITALY

The shining dome of sky over us resembles an inverted glazed, cobalt, china teacup. On the island's maze of cunning paths, soon we're on not a walk but a hike, down, down, down. We reach a precipice—I can see that precipice *is a word I am going to be saying over and over—overlooking a cove that lures you to take a big dive.*

—A Year in the World

When I finish my travels, I will solve the riddle of home. When I finish my travels, I will know the answer.

—A Year in the World

Addresses to Remember

NAME

ADDRESS

NAME   ADDRESS

NAME   **ADDRESS**

NAME   ADDRESS

RECOMMENDED READING

The Sheltering Sky by Paul Bowles

In a Sunburned Country by Bill Bryson

The Gallery by John Horne Burns

Capri and No Longer Capri by Raffaele La Capria

Spain: A History by Raymond Carr

Journey to Alcarria by Camilo José Cela

In Patagonia by Bruce Chatwin

Earthly Paradise by Colette

Torregreca by Ann Cornelisen

Night Letters by Robert Dessaix

Passages from Arabia Deserta by C. M. Doughty

Old Calabria by Norman Douglas

Between the Woods by Patrick Leigh Fermor

Mani by Patrick Leigh Fermor

A Time of Gifts by Patrick Leigh Fermor

The Water by Patrick Leigh Fermor

The Art of Travel by Henry James

Etruscan Places by D. H. Lawrence

Mornings in Mexico by D. H. Lawrence

Sea and Sardinia by D. H. Lawrence

A Season in Granada by Federico García Lorca

Palace Walk by Naguib Mahfouz

Constantinople: City of the World's Desire, 1453–1924
by Philip Mansel

Timeless Cities by David Mayernik

The Ornament of the World by Maria Rosa Menocal

The White Nile by Alan Moorehead

The World by Jan Morris

The World of Venice by Jan Morris

A Traveller in Rome by H. V. Morton

Istanbul by Orhan Pamuk

The Book of Disquiet by Fernando Pessoa

Winter in Majorca by George Sand, translated by Robert Graves

The Wine-Dark Sea by Leonardo Sciascia

The Lycian Shore by Freya Stark

The Valley of the Assassins by Freya Stark

A Winter in Arabia by Freya Stark

Travels with Persephone by Patricia Storace

Journey into Cyprus by Colin Thubron

Crete by Barry Unsworth

The Search for the Etruscan by James Wellard

A Mediterranean Feast by Clifford A. Wright

Books by Frances Mayes

The Discovery of Poetry: A Field Guide to Reading and Writing Poems

Ex Voto

Hours: Lost Roads

Under the Tuscan Sun

Bella Tuscany: The Sweet Life in Italy

In Tuscany

Swan: A Novel

Bringing Tuscany Home: Sensuous Style from the Heart of Italy

A Year in the World: Journeys of a Passionate Traveler

Every Day in Tuscany: Seasons of an Italian Life